In His Sandals

Also by Mother Angelica:

Praying with Mother Angelica
Meditations on the Rosary, the Way of the
Cross, and Other Prayers

Mother Angelica on Christ and Our Lady

Mother Angelica on Suffering and Burnout

Mother Angelica's Quick Guide to the Sacraments

Mother Angelica on Prayer and Living for the Kingdom

Mother Angelica on God, His Home, and His Angels

Mother Angelica's Guide to the Spiritual Life

Mother Angelica's Practical Guide to Holiness

Mother Angelica's Answers, Not Promises

A Holy Hour with Mother Angelica

Living the Scriptures

Mother M. Angelica

In His Sandals
A Journey with Jesus

Edited by Daniel Hopkins

EWTN PUBLISHING, INC.
Irondale, Alabama

EWTN Publishing, Inc.
5817 Old Leeds Road, Irondale, AL 35210

Distributed by Sophia Institute Press, Box 5284, Manchester, NH 03108.

paperback ISBN 978-1-68278-246-0
ebook ISBN 978-1-68278-247-7
Library of Congress Control Number: 2021946719

First printing

Contents

In His Sandals

Part 1

In His Sandals

Chapter 1

We're going to look at the Epistle to the Colossians. So, you run and get your Bible. I'm going to go through some of the Scriptures with you so that these Scriptures become something alive and vibrant, something you live. Just don't memorize them and kind of rattle them off. This is a Book that you live. It's alive! Just as Jesus is Lord and Jesus is alive, so you, as a Christian, must prove to the world that He is Lord and that you are a living being.

Now, when I say "living," I'm not just talking about breathing in and out. I'm talking about *really* living. Most people today exist. Do you just exist? You know, you eat and you sleep and you drink and you work and you do all kinds of things, and then you go to bed at night, get up in the morning, and do the same thing—which is fine. That is what we were created to do.

But there's a lack of purpose in our lives, a lack of goal. We don't find a challenge in our life, and we don't look at life as having a purpose and meaning. You know, if you really want to scare somebody when you meet them, begin to talk about Jesus or Heaven or dying, and they just take off. Next time you get company and they stay too late, you don't have to yawn. Just talk about Heaven, and you watch them. They'll just take off. And yet these people are nine chances out of ten Christian, and it's so difficult to talk about Jesus to Christians.

And yet the first Christians were alive to the Word of God. They spoke of it. They spoke about it a lot! They greeted each other with secret signs because they were persecuted. They had to worship in the catacombs. Well, most people today wouldn't worship at all if they had to fight to worship. They just wouldn't fight.

And so, you and I are not really alive to the beauty of Christianity. And so, in this book, I hope to make this alive for you.

We're going to look at the first chapter of Colossians, and we're going to begin at the ninth verse. We're going to skip over the greeting. You can read that yourself.

And Paul says here, "ever since the day he told us" that one of his disciples gave him the message of the beauty of these Colossians' lives, "we have never failed to pray for you ..." What was the object of Paul's prayers? How did Paul pray for those he loved and those he helped to understand the glory of the Kingdom of Jesus? He said he "asked God that through perfect wisdom and spiritual understanding they would reach a full knowledge of His will." So, in order to understand God's will, St. Paul is saying we need perfect wisdom and spiritual understanding.

Now, what is perfect wisdom? We have very few things perfect. You're not perfect, I'm not perfect, and there's nothing in this world that's perfect. By the very fact that it's on its way out makes it less perfect than it was when it began. So, what is perfect wisdom? Well, that's God's wisdom, and the Christian has that ability to see God in the present moment, to see His wisdom in the present moment.

You know, it's really exciting to watch God work in the present moment. But if you're not aware of God in that moment, if everything to you is chance and luck, and you do it or your neighbor does it, you're always at the mercy of something outside your control. And so, you're like a reed shaken by the wind. And Paul is saying you need perfect wisdom and only God has perfect wisdom. Your wisdom and my wisdom are imperfect. You know, that's why you and I don't understand why things happen to us.

Have you ever said, "I don't understand God's will. I don't know why He permits this in my life or permitted this in someone else's life"? And we don't understand it. Maybe five or six years later, maybe twenty years later, you look back on your life and you suddenly find out that something very, very good happened. I learn this every day.

You know, sometimes I begin something, and it just seems to go to pot; it just seems to fall apart. And immediately, the thought comes to my mind: *God is at work*. And you just watch Him put the pieces together.

You have a disappointment in your life. Instead of getting frustrated and antagonistic toward your neighbor and God and feeling guilty, say, "God, You bring good out of it." This is hope. Hope is that magnificent virtue that makes you, as a Christian, see good in everything.

Now, we don't understand it, but we know God's wisdom is with us. I love to look at Jesus in the morning when I get up in faith and say, "Jesus, I know there'll be a lot of things today that happen to me or to those I love, just ordinary things—a machine breaks down or just a lot of things—and I will not understand it. But I want to give them to You because I see Your perfect wisdom." And then you begin suddenly to understand the realities of life. You begin to live in a life that's both visible and invisible. You begin to see God's providence.

Didn't He say not a sparrow falls that He doesn't see and that every hair on your head is counted? Well, then, if He understands and wills and permits and sees all these insignificant things—there's nothing more insignificant than your hair; of course, some of you are getting bald, and I bet that is very significant to you, but really it isn't—how much more is He going to take care of those important things in your life? He is not going to let one thing happen to you. The secret is that you understand this, and that's why Paul was praying for these Colossians. He says, "I ask God that through perfect wisdom and spiritual understanding ..."

Now, you know, you and I, as Christians, we may have a lot of understanding. But it's worldly! Now, I'm not saying there's anything wrong with being in the world. You and I are in the world. God put us here, and we are to work out, with His grace, our salvation. But we are not to be of the world. And so our understanding must be totally different from anyone else's. We must understand how God works, why He permits suffering, why children are so unhappy today. We must want to do something about it. It's a kind of discernment.

You know, so many of us don't have discernment. We can be in the midst of evil and never understand because we don't have spiritual understanding. All we want is what we can eat and drink, and we want all the comfort in the world. We don't want to be responsible for anything, so we don't really put in a good day's work. We're not faithful because we don't have the spiritual understanding. We don't understand that everything I do for God — if I pick up a pin for the love of Jesus, if I sweep a floor and do dishes, simple things.

Men that go out and make a living — and it's hard to make a living today because you work and you work, and you work hard, and you have all the things taken off your pay that they need to take off, and you come home, and inflation goes up, and you're frustrated. And so it's hard. It's hard to live in the world. And yet the Christian has to have a spiritual understanding. This understanding of things that happen is so much more elevated than it is for the person who does not know God. You and I, as Christians, need this spiritual understanding of everything that happens to us, and this spiritual understanding means that you and I see God in everything that happens. That's faith — to see God. And hope is to look at a situation, be it painful or joyful. So I have to see God in joy, too.

You know, one of the most terrible things in the world among Christians, I think, is a kind of spirit of ingratitude. Oh, we ask God for all kinds of things. But we never thank Him. It looks like when we're in trouble, God is supposed to take us out. But when we have a success, we did it. And so, there's no one to thank. We just enjoy the whole thing.

This is a terrible imbalance. There's no understanding there. There's no kind of wisdom, because we attribute good to ourselves; we attribute evil to the world, and God somehow, the Big Daddy up there, just takes us out.

God and you work together! God and you are working together in the present moment. God permits and ordains that moment, gives you the strength and courage, gives you grace, that part of Himself that makes you overcome whatever is difficult for you. And God looks at you in that present moment, and He expects great things from you, not little things.

We have a great God, and you are called to be great. You are called to change this world, and more than that—you are called to transform this world! If you don't transform it, first by doing your own transforming—what I mean is you cooperate with God's grace so that your life is totally changed—if you don't do that and, by that example, transform your neighbor, then you and I are going to have to answer to God for the world we live in. When we die, we're going to have to admit that we were not the Christians He desired us to be.

And St. Paul goes on here and he says, "so you will be able to lead the kind of life which the Lord expects of you" (Colossians 1:10).

You see, to see things—your loneliness, your heart-aches, your pain, your frustrations of life, the anxieties of life, the joys, the ecstasies, the beautiful days, the beautiful moments, the loving moments—to see all of this in the eyes of God and to see God within it all is to have spiritual understanding. So that in trial and suffering you do not lose hope, so that when things happen to you that you do not understand, you maintain a high faith level.

So that when people come toward you or with you, or you work with them or live with them who are difficult to love—when that happens, you want to run away, you feel so empty inside, so lonely—then you will be filled with a love that comes from God, a kind of love that is like God's love because you have God's love within you. And so, rather than being in the world expecting to be fed, you feed your neighbor. This is a spiritual understanding. This is what God expects from you. He's saying here the reason you need to know what God wants you to do as a Christian is so you can lead the life He expects from you.

Today, you wonder if anyone knows the Ten Commandments. You know, it's amazing how we manipulate the Scriptures, how we kind of explain man to God, how we excuse immorality, permissiveness, rudeness, lack of love, coldness, indifference, hardness of heart. We excuse ourselves. Oh, we can even quote Scripture, God forgive us! Just imagine how far we have really gone from what God expects us to be. Why is that? Because we don't pray. Do you notice St. Paul says, "I pray for you every day for these beautiful gifts," these gifts that are so important to you and to me, to this whole world? You can help this world.

In another passage, St. Paul says, "This is a wicked generation, and your lives should redeem it." Well, we all know that Jesus redeemed us. We all know that it is only through His Precious Blood we are redeemed. And yet St. Paul says, "This is a wicked generation." And every generation is wicked in its own way. Our generation is no different from ages of the past. And yet you and I are to be such beacons on top of a mountain, such a light that the world will get hope. The world will see something so good and so wonderful in you that they would say, "Hey, there is more to life, and I'm getting out of it! There's more to being a Christian!"

It's exciting to be a Christian, and we've made Christianity such a religion that all you really need to do to be a Christian today is just go to church, and that's all. And in between Sunday and Sunday, you can almost do as you please and excuse it. And God is saying, "No, you can't do that. I expect you to be great. I expect you to be different. I expect this Book [the Bible] to be written in your life for all men to read." Just imagine!

St. Paul said, "You are an ambassador of Christ. Your life is a letter to the world." You know, a letter is something someone writes to you. Their thoughts are put on paper, and they convey their feelings to you by a little piece of paper and ink. Well, this [the Bible] is paper and ink. But the message, the Word of God, is more than a letter. It's a power, and that power must be so great in you that it shows.

You know, you can't be happy and sad at the same time. If you're happy, it shows. If you're a loving person, it shows. Did you ever see an angry person look gentle? That's an impossibility. Did you ever see a person full of hate look loving? No. It can't be.

But why is it, then, if these are impossible contradictions, that we can be a Christian in name and not in deed? Why is it we can be a Christian in thought and not in action? When you boil it down, it doesn't make sense. So then, there must be something wrong with our concepts, with our spiritual understanding and our concept of wisdom, something wrong with how you and I live with God.

You know, some people think that to live with God in this life, you're called to be a minister or a religious like myself or a priest or somebody up on a pedestal. In other words, to be holy is to be called. Well, if you were born and you're listening to me, then you are called to be holy!

Jesus said, "It is the Father's will that all men be saved." Now, you must understand that and especially when you profess to be a Christian. Every time you go into a church, you know what you're doing? You're telling everyone in that church, you're telling everyone that passes the street, that's driving down the road seeing you walk in, that "I am a Christian."

You know, in the days of the first Christians, if anyone got caught going into the catacombs, it was because they weren't careful and maybe a soldier would see them sneaking into the catacombs, and he would go to Nero or Diocletian and he'd say, "I saw So-and-so going into the catacombs. He is a Christian."

In fact, that's what the maidservant in the courtyard told Peter. She said, "Your speech betrays you." Peter had a Galilean accent. His whole demeanor betrayed him as a follower of Jesus. So, you have to have some kind of telling sign about you. This is what God expects from you and me, a kind of love that just flows out of us.

When you relegate Christianity only to a religion and you can satisfy that obligation and then go your way, how many Christians lie and cheat in their business and take advantage of other people and are nasty and rude? You see, these don't go together any more than a loving hateful person. You can't be loving and hateful. And so, St. Paul is saying God expects something from you, and he goes on. He says, "a life acceptable to him in all its aspects." Oh, now this is something else! Some of us decided we're going to be good in one aspect of our life, so we're going to do a lot of things. And now business: "Well, you know, you can be worldly in business, because if you don't, they're going to eat you up."

But St. Paul is saying God wants you to be a Christian in *all* aspects of your life. You can't decide which aspect of life you're going to be a Christian in. You're either a whole Christian everywhere, or I don't think you're Christian at all. Now, that doesn't mean that you and I are always going to be perfect. There are no perfect people in this earth! But what it does mean is that you strive and you have a perception of what's right. You have a feeling. You have a conscience that stirs up when you make a mistake.

It means that when you do sin or make a mistake, you are quick to repent. It means that you have a beautiful effort, that you're always striving to be better. It means that you have compassion on your brother because your brother is a sinner and so are you. You're a sinner, I'm a sinner, we're all sinners. And because we all have weaknesses and we're all struggling and we're all fighting to be good, to be what God expects us to be, we have that compassion on our brother.

So, being the kind of Christian Paul is talking about is not to go around perfect and not to go around condemning everyone and judging everyone. It means that you strive, and though you fall, you rise immediately and strive again. It means that you try to learn what these Christian principles are so you can adapt them to your daily life. And today, it's very, very hard, because the whole world is saying to you, "Eat, drink, and be merry, for tomorrow you die, and there's nothing else."

And you sometimes have to stand alone. You have to stand alone and say, "No, there is more! The greatest is to come!" That's what God expects from you.

St. Paul says, "showing the results in all the good actions you do and increasing your knowledge of God" (verses 10–11).

You show these inner beautiful concepts and principles; you manifest them in your daily life. For example, if I had an opportunity to be angry—and I did, as I have a lot of opportunities—and I decide that instead of being angry like myself, that's me, I'm going to be like Jesus. What happens to me when I make that kind of choice in my life? That means that, in that effort to be gentle, though I feel angry, I have acquired knowledge of God. That's not hard to understand.

You know, some people think that you ought to just act the way you feel because that's honesty. No, it's not honesty. If we're all going to act the way we feel, we'll be a bunch of animals shortly. Because Jesus says to us to be gentle, and there's no one on this earth who feels gentle all the time.

So, that means there's a choice to make. To do God's will is to choose to be something I don't want to be at that moment.

Chapter 2

The divinity of Jesus — the God-Man, the Second Person of the Holy Trinity, was always up in the heights. And so, in this particular Epistle, 1 John 4:7, if you have your Scripture with you, He's saying, "My dear people, let us love one another since love comes from God." And He says, "Everyone who loves is begotten by God and knows God."

We know that the Eternal Word, Jesus, the Word Made Flesh Who dwelt among us, is begotten by God. So, you and I are begotten by God.

Do you realize your dignity? Do you understand how valuable you are to the world and to God Himself? You are God's treasure, a treasure that He planted on this earth for a particular purpose. And that's why, wherever you are, you must radiate that love through which you came into this world. Love created you, and He created you to love and to be loved. This is the crying need of every individual in the world. We need to be needed. Everyone needs to be needed.

Do you ever wonder why retired people sometimes die very soon after retirement? Not everyone, and I don't want all of you that just retired to begin to wonder when you're going to die, but it does happen frequently. Is it because they no longer feel needed or loved?

You see, God has planted these desires in our hearts so that we will seek Him and seek the good of our neighbor. He didn't just plant us like we plant a seed in the ground and say, "Okay, now. Grow. Do what you can."

And He doesn't look down on us and say, "You miserable creatures. I'm sorry I created you. What are you doing down there?"

No! He looks at you tenderly, like a real father, because He is a real Father. So, you have been begotten by God, Who is Love.

Why? Why did God create you? Out of a possible eighty billion people who might have been created in this world, why did He choose you to be? Well, we really don't know. Someone asked me that not too long ago, and I said, "Well, I guess He's got bad taste."

I think sometimes He does, perhaps. Because you and I can really give Him the glory. Because of our weaknesses and our frailties, we can glorify Him. Because when we love unselfishly, the world's going to know there is a power within us greater than ourselves.

And John says, "Anyone who fails to love can never have known God" (verse 8). See, God is Love. And when you do not love, not only are you miserable, not only do you make everyone around you miserable, but you do not know God. To know God is to experience God, and every time you love, you are experiencing God Himself. God is Love! And that love for your neighbor must be pure. When I say pure, I'm talking about unselfish love, without a thought for yourself.

And he goes on: "We must do this *because God is Love*." You and I possess love, but God *is* Love. God is Goodness. You and I may possess goodness. We may possess patience. We may possess a certain serenity or calmness. We may possess a certain kind of sweetness or kindness. You may be trusting. You may be just a lot of good things. But when we possess these things, God is all of this. Isn't it tremendous? God is all of these. He's everything I want to be!

Sometimes, I've had a kind of hard day, and at the end of the day, I feel just tense, frustrated—where you wish you could start the day over again. Maybe you wish you had stayed in bed that day. Have you ever had one of those days? Well, when I have one of those days, I go to our little chapel, and I sit there, and I just look at Jesus. And I just close my eyes and begin to absorb the very thing I need. God is in that chapel. God is around me, and those of you at home can do it in your living room because God is wherever you are. You can just close your eyes for a few moments.

If you feel angry, for example, or someone has hurt you, and all day long you fault this anger and you want so much not to be angry. Your will does not want to be angry, but inside you, it's just going around and around and around and around, and you're just angry—bitter, almost. You don't want to feel that way. And all the efforts that you have exerted have just been a failure.

Well, the next time you have one of those days, you just go somewhere where it's quiet. Sometimes, you can go out into the woods, where God's nature is so overwhelming, and you can just be aware of God and His silent, awesome presence. And that silent, awesome presence is His Love, and that Love is always healing. And when you are in great need, if your soul is all disturbed with anger or bitterness or resentfulness or rejection or regrets, whatever it is, you are in need of being healed.

And there's only one thing that can heal you, and that's Jesus. The only One that can heal you is God. The only One that can effect any kind of change in you is the Spirit—that beautiful Sanctifier Who is your Friend Who lives in your heart. If you know Jesus and you're repentant and in grace, you have that Divine Indwelling. And St. John promises that to us. He says, "God's love for us was revealed when God sent into the world his only Son.... This is the love I mean: not our love for God, but God's love for us" (verses 9–10).

See, most of us are all twisted around, worrying about how much we love God. We wonder sometimes, "Do I love God at all?" We judge by our feelings. We say, "Well, I don't feel God. I don't feel like I love Him."

But He never asks us to feel. He asked us to do His will. And so, when you have those frustrating days, when you feel rejected by your neighbor and unloved by God, you must use faith, because the revelation Jesus has given us tells us that God loves us always. And His love is so deep that though we reject Him sometimes, He never, never, never will reject us. Even if one chooses to go to Hell, it is a personal choice. God does not send people to Hell. They reject Him. They turn around and go the other way. So, God's love is constant and faithful.

God loves you. And when you keep His commandments, He lives in you. And when you feel frustrated, you need to sit in God's presence, because God is everything you and I are not. And so, when I am in need of God's gentleness or patience or serenity, I just go to Him, close my eyes, and become very, very much aware of that silent, healing presence. You can do that right now.

Wherever you are, why don't you just close your eyes for a few moments and just become very, very much aware of that beautiful, awesome presence of God very, very deep in the center of your soul? So deep that you just feel, you just become aware of a tremendous amount of love around you. So much love that you hardly remember what was wrong with you. All the anger begins to go, all the resentfulness, all the rejection that you feel, all that bitterness. You begin to feel—I don't mean emotionally feel—but I want you to be aware of something that is. I'm not trying to excite your emotions, because that's something temporary. I'm trying to put you in a depth of faith so deep and so great that you become aware of something that always is, and that is the healing presence of God's love for you.

And when this chapter is over, I want you to put yourself again in that beautiful, awesome presence and know that whatever is wrong with you, whatever rebellion is in your soul, whatever heartache in your mind, whatever disappointment, whatever sickness, whatever is in you that's causing you to wonder and to question God's love for you, the only way you're going to ever understand that love is to place yourself in that beautiful presence around you.

He is here now, He is there in your living room, and He is there for one purpose—to save you, and this is what St. John is saying here. It's not my love for God that's important; it's that God loves me. Listen to this again. It's worth repeating many times over, and this is verse 10 of chapter 4, St. John's First Epistle.

He says, "This is the love I mean." He's trying to make this very important to you. We say, "What kind of love?" He says, "The love I mean is not our love for God, but God's love for us when He sent His Son to be the Sacrifice that takes our sins away." He says, "My dear people, since God has loved us so much, we too should love one another" (verse 11).

You see what happens, and perhaps you experienced that in those few seconds that we were speaking of that beautiful, silent presence, that healing presence. Once you begin to live in God's love, then that love permeates your being and goes right through you, penetrates you. And suddenly that love begins to go out. It is a force; it is a power. And that love is such a power. Not only does it heal you; it heals your relationships with your neighbor, your family, your friends, your loved ones, your husband, your wife.

God is constantly healing. His love is always healing. That's why a Christian is called by God to witness to the love He has for mankind. And this witness is a healing witness because the world is in constant daily need of being healed.

You know, when we think of healing, we're always talking about physical healing. But Our Lord said, "Don't worry about that. Rather to go into the Kingdom with one eye, one arm, one leg than somewhere else with two arms and two legs and two eyes." See, we understand how Jesus thinks about the body. And though He wants us to pray to be healed in body, it is much more important that my soul is constantly healed. Because you and I, even at our best, are always imperfect in some way or another.

And Scripture tells us that God finds imperfections even in the angels. So, we're not trying to be a perfect people. We are trying to be a repentant, humble people—a people who are willing to acknowledge a need for God! And that need is so great that we're not ashamed to wait upon His mercy, to sit there as one in need and absorb the very thing I need.

If you are angry, for example, kind of even-tempered, always mad, and you want to get over that, and you've worked at it for years and years and years, you seem to get nowhere fast, and no one really understands that you are working on it. Then sometimes when you pray, instead of just saying, "God, make me gentle or keep me from being angry," just place yourself in the presence of the Gentle God, this Gentleness. Begin to absorb this gentle Man, because you are in that presence.

When you are in the sun, you absorb the rays of the sun. When you are in that presence, you absorb that presence. And when your soul is filled with His grace, where the Indwelling is within you—when the Father, the Son, and the Spirit live within your heart—you are in that presence.

You have merely to close your eyes wherever you are and be aware of that presence. And that healing presence will take hold of you. And all the anger will begin to ebb away. All the frustration will begin to ebb away. All that tension that you feel that makes you angry, that you blame other people for, you will suddenly begin to understand and control—all because you are more and more aware of your having been begotten by God, Who is Love.

Let's look at St. John again. He says, "God will live in us, and His love will be complete in us. We can know we are living in Him and He is living in us because He lets us share His Spirit" (verses 12–13).

You see, God has made you a son and God must look upon us with great love; otherwise, He would have never even desired to give us such a gift — divine adoption. This means that you and I have within us the very Spirit of God. I can say, "Abba, Father!" and mean it. It's not a pretend situation. I really mean it, because He has given me Himself.

"Grace is a participation," St. Peter says, "in the divine nature." So, you and I are a real part of God, and we know that by the fact that St. John says that He has given you and me that Spirit. We must live in that Spirit. We must be aware of the power of that Spirit. And that power is reaching out into the world today. That power is in you, and that power wants to come out of you and touch your neighbor and say, "Hey! There is a God! That God is with us! That God is full of joy! That God is powerful! There is no power on this earth as great as our God is powerful. There is no situation on this earth that He cannot solve, that He cannot help."

This whole world, be it ever so evil, be it ever so wicked, can change because the power of Our God is omnipotent. It is without limit. God only needs you to manifest that power in your soul. And He wants you to constantly share in that power so He can go out to your neighbor. And so, He is saying, "We ourselves saw and testified that the Father sent His Son as Savior of the world." And you have to prove that.

"If anyone acknowledges that Jesus is the Son of God, God remains in him and he in God" (verse 15). The one who loves and loves much—we can be assured that God lives in him and he lives in God. And St. Paul says, "We ourselves have known and put our faith in God's love toward ourselves" (verse 16).

Do you have faith in God's love for you? Do you really believe that? I don't mean an intellectual assent to that beautiful truth. I mean believe that with all your heart so that it is part and parcel of your daily life. Because St. John goes on. He says, "God is Love, and anyone who lives in love lives in God and God lives in him."

Did you hear that? God is Love, and anyone who lives in love lives in God and God lives in him. So, the whole world is going to judge your Christianity by the amount of love that you have for your neighbor.

And he says, "In love there can be no fear" (verse 18). You see, if you are living in that awesome, silent presence—if you keep placing yourself in that presence and you become more and more aware of that power, the power of that presence, and that presence takes hold of you and constantly heals you—when you are aware of that and you live in that presence, then all men are going to know that you and God live as one. They're going to understand that you know God, that you experience God. Because everywhere they go, every time they see you, every time they see other Christians like you, they will experience God. It's like God giving Himself to God.

When I love you and you love me, when we are loving each other because we are constantly experiencing this love of God in our hearts and our souls and our minds, then all men will know there is a God; all men will know that God is Love.

Right now, men question that God is Love, because people are so cruel to one another, so demanding, so unjust, so prejudiced.

When men act like animals instead of sons of God, when men degrade themselves, when there is no longer charity or kindness or respect, when rudeness lives and reigns and fear takes hold, then there is no love. And St. John assures us of this because he says, "Fear is driven out by perfect love … and anyone who is afraid is still imperfect in love" (verse 18).

We're afraid of our neighbor and afraid to live and afraid to die. If we're afraid of yesterday and afraid of tomorrow, we are imperfect in love. We have not put ourselves often enough, if at all, in that silent presence in the depths of our soul.

You may close your eyelids and say, "Well, all I see is darkness."

That's not darkness. It's such a brightness, it's such a light, that you cannot see because when you are in that state of grace, God lives in you and you have no need to be afraid, either of yesterday or tomorrow. You have no need to be afraid of anything or anyone. And when anger and rebellion and resentment and regret and disappointment seem to take hold of you with their icy grip, when they seem to possess you to the point where you cannot breathe except in utter frustration, then you just place yourself and all of your needs in that presence and close your eyes and let that Spirit within you and the Father Who loves you and the Son Who redeemed you and came down especially for you—let them take possession of that soul that's so distressed and so unhappy. Just let that need for God, that need to be delivered and healed, be your prayer.

Just close your eyes and become very much aware of His presence, that healing, loving presence. And begin to experience in your soul, through the power of that Spirit, gentleness, kindness, compassion, goodness, trustfulness, patience, love, joy—those beautiful fruits of the Spirit mentioned in Galatians.

God wants you to have all these good things. He wants you to experience His love more and more so that you can give that love to your neighbor. And that neighbor, who perhaps has a hard time believing there is a God, when he sees you receive and sees the love and light in your life, says, "Truly, there is a God."

Chapter 3

We're going to look at the Epistle of St. James. St. James is a kind of hard man. We know that Peter and Paul had a time with St. James. St. James was a man who could kind of get to the core of a matter. And he was very blunt, a man that told it like it is, a loving man — a man who adhered to the law and to the Good News. He knew Jesus was Lord, and if he were here today, he'd say, "Get with it!" He would look at you and me and say, "How come, if you're such a wonderful Christian or you profess to be a Christian, how come your life and your profession are not the same?"

I think he'd say that to me, too, because no matter how good a Christian we are, we do have some areas where we're just a little vacillating, don't we?

We don't need to feel bad about that. We just need to do something about it. And so, we're going to begin with the very first part of St. James's Epistle, and here's what it says: "My brothers, you will always have your trials" (James 1:2). That doesn't seem very encouraging, does it? But that's reality, and some people think Christianity is just one big whoop-de-do! You know, kind of joy, joy, joy! Well, it is joy. It's not always happiness.

Happiness is something that comes from things outside of me. If someone gave me a gift, it would make me happy. But the very fact that that gift made me happy shows that I was dependent for that kind of happiness upon the decision, the goodwill, of someone else, that someone who decided to give me a gift. My happiness is dependent, then, upon exterior things, things outside of me, things that happened to me that I am happy about, that make me feel good or benefit me or render me a service.

But joy is something else. Joy is something that wells up within us. It is something God Himself has given us. "My joy I give to you," Jesus said, "and no man takes it away," because it's entirely upon Jesus.

St. James says, "Try to treat [trials] as a happy privilege" (verse 3). Now, that's a little bit difficult. That's asking a lot! Do you see how St. James is very demanding? But he's only demanding because he knows a little of the glory that is to come. And so, as we are distinguishing the difference between joy and happiness, and we just said that happiness comes from outside of us, we always look upon good things as the cause of happiness—you give me a gift, you do something nice for me, the weather is beautiful, something good.

Now, St. James is saying trials are a happy privilege. I don't think you and I have come that far, have we? I mean, trials are something we want to get rid of as soon as possible. We pray to God most fervently when we have a trial, when we're trying to get rid of a pain or a suffering.

And here's St. James. I mean, what is it with him? I am to treat a trial, an occasion to be patient or kind or understanding, as a happy privilege. In other words, what is there, then, in some particular occasion that really calls for great patience or compassion—someone that is ill—what is it that calls forth for me a kind of happiness?

Well, it's the opportunity. See, an unspiritual person only sees what's happening at the moment, and that can be pretty bad sometimes. And although we feel within ourselves a kind of boiling, still there must come to our mind a deeper reality. And that reality is that this is a chance to be like Jesus. We don't always take it. We don't always grab that chance, and that's because we don't see it as a happy privilege.

Do you know what a privilege is? It's something special. It's an opportunity that isn't given to everyone. Now, St. James is saying you and I should look upon the trials and the happenings of daily life as something special. Well, I don't know about you, but all I want to do is get rid of them. As far as I'm concerned, I could say, "Well, I could do without them." And I think you think that, too. But that only says that you and I have not reached that kind of Christianity that St. James expects of us, that Jesus expects of us. He must say, and he is saying to you and to myself, "Jesus is giving you something special in this trial. It's a happy privilege to be like Jesus. It's an opportunity to be like God."

Wouldn't it be wonderful if you and I thought that way all the time? At least some of the time?

Wouldn't that take the edge off something that happens to you? Wouldn't that take the resentment or the guilt or the regrets? Oh, the unforgiving spirit in most of us—someone does something to us, and we just can't forgive. You know, forgiveness is so important in our lives as Christians that Jesus demanded that we forgive seventy times seven times a day! Just imagine how important forgiveness is. He knows that we're always going to have occasions to commit faults, imperfections. Frailties are always going to come out. There are no perfect people in this world. And that's why He demanded that we have that disposition of soul and that compassion that as we look upon these opportunities as happy privileges, we can turn them into good, and that is forgiveness.

You and I need forgiveness from God many, many, many times a day. And so, if I am the recipient of God's forgiveness, you and I must forgive each other. And sometimes when somebody rattles your nerves, especially your kids sometimes when they're yelling and screaming and you really yell at them a lot louder and harder than they deserve for what they did, I think you need to just say, "Look, I'm sorry. I blew my stack."

You know, if we were honest with ourselves and those around us, I think we'd have a lot more understanding. We're human beings. Parents can fail, children fail, friends fail, but that's part of being human. It is divine to forgive. It is human to fall and divine to forgive and go on like nothing happened. That's freedom! And I think that's why St. James is calling trials a "happy privilege."

You look at forgiveness in your life as a Christian. You really can't be like Jesus. You can't even begin if there's anyone in your life you haven't forgiven. Forgiveness is so important. It makes us so much like God so quickly. You know, we all have a hard time loving like God loves.

That's the commandment, but God loves all the time, and He loves you as you are, and He loves you even when you're not very nice. And I find that hard, and I know you find it hard to love like that. But the quickest way you and I can be like God is in forgiving — it's not the easiest way. But this Book is not easy! And if you make it easy, you're not living it.

There's such a great difference between the world and this Book, because the world says, "If you have trials, get rid of them." The world says, "If somebody bothers you, leave." The world is a total opposite. The world just strives to give you pleasure, to give you everything you want, all the comfort you want. Isn't it strange, though, that we live in an age when there are so many comforts and yet so few happy people?

And here is St. James saying that trials are a happy privilege. Wouldn't that be a freedom? Oh, that would be fantastic! You and I could look at all our life with all its heartaches and trials and disappointments instead of hanging on to them, and some of you have some things in your life you hang on to for years! That's pretty bad, because you see, it's like a cancer. It's like a hidden disease. It warps your soul. Physical diseases can come and go, and you can do something about them because you feel them, you see them. But spiritual diseases, sometimes you don't see. You're so immersed in hatred, you're so immersed in an unforgiving spirit, so immersed in coldness or resentment that you don't see it's eating you up. And so, St. James's solution to this kind of problem was to look at all these trials as opportunities to be like Jesus.

And he goes and he says, "You understand that your faith is only put to the test to make you patient" (verse 3). You know, we ought to write that down on a little piece of paper and say that "trial is to make us understand that faith is put to the test to make us patient."

Do you know what that's really saying? Well, it's saying that God permits many, many things in your life and my life to make us patient. You know, I can't be patient if I don't have an opportunity.

Now, it is not easy to be patient. I don't know about you, but I find it very difficult. Sometimes I wake up in the morning and I'm not out of bed and I'm impatient already. I can't find the light.

I'll tell you something that happened to me the other day that was so frustrating and so small! I somehow or other must have thrown my arm out of the covers the other night, and I bumped up against a glass of water on my stand, and the water went everywhere. And my rosary and everything I had — my crucifix — was just soaking in water.

And my first thought was: *"Eeeeek!"*

Now, two o'clock in the morning, water everywhere! So, I got some tissues, and some of the tissues that you get today I think the devil's in them. You know, it looks like they don't want you to get them out of the box. It looks like there's an invisible hand at the bottom of the box keeping them from getting out of the box. They put them in a box, and then they put some kind of heavy plastic all over the hole. And when you try to pull one of these tissues out, it just doesn't come out.

And there I am at two o'clock in the morning, trying to pull these tissues out to sop up all this running water, and it was terrible! I thought to myself, "There you are, Angelica, angry and impatient." I thought, "Oh, how small it was in the middle of the night, just an insignificant thing."

But it showed me that the old woman is still here, that the old person with all the effort is still there. And I wasn't discouraged. I looked at Jesus, and I said, "Thank You, Jesus. There I go again. But now I have an opportunity to be like You." So, I laboriously extracted the tissues and sopped up the water. And then with sopping Kleenex in my hand, I had to go around finding a wastebasket.

These are significant things, but it did me a great service. It showed me that I am not like Jesus yet. But it also showed me I have the privilege. It also gave me an opportunity to be humbled by the fact that I knew I am still an angry person inside. It gave me an opportunity to change and more than change — to be transformed, to say to myself, "I don't think Jesus would get all excited over a little glass of water falling over. I think that if He did, He would look at the Father and say, 'Thank You, Father, for this opportunity.'"

I began to know God. I began to know goodness, because suddenly, when I put myself in His beautiful presence alone in my room, that beautiful presence of God with me and God in me gave me that grace, that opportunity, that beautiful chance, that privilege to turn something not good into something very, very good.

Now, this is a small thing, and yet many big things happen in my life and your life, big choices that you have to make. And some of you get angry with God and you say, "God, You shouldn't put me in this position."

But really, He didn't. You put yourself into it. His power is within you. His grace is within you. The strength to overcome is with you, no matter what your weakness is. There is no weakness greater than God's power. And that power is right there, ready for you to hang on to, to hold on to, and to use.

That's a beautiful, beautiful consolation to know that you're not alone. And no matter how down you are or how bad you are, no matter how far you've fallen, you can always rise. You look at it and say, "Well, here my life has been one big mess, but I can use that as a happy privilege. I can use it to be humble. I can use it to manifest God's Mercy in my life."

Don't you feel overjoyed when you see a sinner who repents and begins to turn his life over to Jesus? Doesn't that just stir your heart? Well, why don't you be that sinner?

You say, "Well, I'm not a big sinner. I'm good." Well, you can be better. If you're good, you can be holy. And if you possess a tremendous amount of holiness, then you can possess that much more! There is no limit to the good you can become. You are called by God to be like God, and that is such a dignity.

We're going to look at St. James again. He says, "But he must ask with faith, and no trace of doubt, because a person who has doubts is like the waves thrown up in the sea when the wind drives. That sort of person, in two minds, wavering between going different ways, must not expect that the Lord will give him anything" (verses 5–7).

Do you know what I call these kinds of people? I call them "popover Christians." They're a little bit in this kingdom and a little bit in that kingdom, one day they're good and the next day terrible. All their life, just popping over from one kingdom to another, just like that — it's terrible. There's an emptiness inside.

Are you like that? Do you have that emptiness inside of your soul, and you just don't know what to do with it? You try this and it doesn't satisfy you, and you do this, and you're still unhappy, and you do that, and there's always that gnawing vacuum. That's the Lord, and that's a good sign. If you have that vacuum in you, you rejoice, because God is hounding you, and He's saying, "I don't want you to have two minds. I want you to have a mind like Mine. I want you to be like Me."

Jesus says, "Be like I am." "Learn of Me," He said, "for I am meek and humble of heart." He said, "Be compassionate like the Father is compassionate." And then, in order that you and I can be like the Holy Spirit, He said, "Love as God loves with the love of the Spirit."

See how you are called to be great? So, no matter how weak you are, how frail, no matter what your sins are or were, you just put them in the mercy of God, and you begin right now to live, not only a good life, but a holy life. You rise above yourself. Don't you have two minds. You look at life in a way different than anyone else. You begin to look at life and yourself and your neighbor as a child of God with great dignity.

This is what St. James is saying here. He's saying that you and I must be aware of our dignity as Christians. We must be aware of how much we are loved by God. Do you know how much God loves you? Does your neighbor know how much God loves you? Does he know it by your joy? Does he know it by the way you accept the trials of this life? Does he know it by how you forgive your neighbor? I think that's the scandal of Christianity today — a lack of love, first among Christians and then toward our families and the lack of forgiveness. That's one of the worst scandals in the world today.

So, if there's anyone in your family, in your relationship, if there is anyone at all in this whole wide world that you have not forgiven, will you now? Will you just look at Jesus on the Cross or in your heart? Would you look at Him as a Resurrected Lord manifesting to you the glory that is to come? Will you look at all of the times He has forgiven you and say to others, "I forgive you," and look upon the opportunity to forgive as that happy privilege?

You know, several times in Our Lord's life, He forgave sin, and people didn't even ask for forgiveness. For example, the man that was kind of lowered down through the roof. Jesus just looked at him and He said, "Your sins are forgiven you." The man hadn't asked for forgiveness, at least not that I remember.

On the Cross, Jesus said, "Father, forgive them, for they know not what they do," and yet you don't hear anyone asking for forgiveness. Now, that doesn't mean you can't ask or shouldn't ask. You must ask for forgiveness from your neighbor and from God, because unless you ask, you cannot be forgiven! But it does show Jesus is manifesting to us, first, the source of our unhappiness is an unforgiving heart, and He had a loving heart. And it also manifests to you and me His readiness to forgive.

He looked upon us; He looked upon the men of His time as weak human beings. He knew what was in them. He knew their very thoughts. He knew their hearts. And His heart was always open. The gate of His heart is always open to forgive. It's an attitude. It's an attribute. It is God Himself. It is divine to forgive. And you and I, as Christians, imitators of Jesus — that's what we are — you and I, as Christians, must have an open heart, because to forgive is to love. It is a divine way of loving to say, "I forgive you. I love you." It is to look upon the opportunity to forgive as something happy, as a privilege.

We are so hurt, and we are so concerned about ourselves and our feelings, and we're so concerned about justice and injustice. We're so concerned about our own dignity and filled with human respect that we are bogged down by a lack of understanding of the real essence of a trial as a happy privilege to be like Jesus.

So, the next time something happens to you that you find difficult, or someone offends you or aggravates you, don't look upon it so much as a personal insult. Look upon it like Jesus, with an open heart.

St. Paul told us to forgive as soon as an argument begins. That's pretty quick, isn't it? Look upon all the trials in your life, and even upon those who have caused them, through the wisdom of God. Look upon them as a happy privilege. Look upon them as an opportunity to be like God and to experience the love, that pure, holy, unselfish love—the kind that forgives, the kind that looks upon the present moment as something precious.

You and I always would like to, in many areas, start all over. Well, you have that opportunity right now. Do not let the sun go down on your anger or your unforgiving spirit. And if the person you want to forgive will not accept it, just pray for them as long as your heart is a forgiving heart, as long as you see merely opportunities to forgive.

This is very important to you as a Christian. It's important to the world, for unless the world sees you as a Christian, it will not believe.

God bless you, and be loving today.

Part 2

Our Hermitage

Chapter 4

We're going to look at a part of Scripture in St. John's Gospel that we ordinarily look at during Lent. And of course, that's a good time to look at it, but this is a part of Scripture that is very, very necessary for daily life, and we need to look at it often during the year. It's the Last Supper Discourse, but the part we want to take in today is the very first part of chapter 13.

It says, "It was before the festival of the Passover, and Jesus knew that the hour had come for Him to pass from this world to the Father. He had always loved those who were His in the world, but now He showed how perfect His love was" (John 13:1).

Here is an incident where Jesus is manifesting how perfect His love is. I want you to keep that sentence in mind, because you would think that when He came as a man, a child, and was born in a cold, cold cave and ran away from a terrible ruler, and He lived as a carpenter, when He didn't have a place to lay His head, when He was hungry and thirsty, that He manifested His love. And He certainly did, many, many times. But now, it says here He showed how perfect His love was. Absolutely perfect. In other words, there was nothing left undone. Jesus used every opportunity that came His way to show you and me how much He loved us.

The love that does not manifest itself is no love at all. If someone never tells you they love you or they never do anything nice for you, they never smile at you, they never say a kind word, you have every reason to believe that this person does not love you.

Love must be manifested. It must be shown. You can't love anyone and never show it. That kind of love is no love at all, because love is a power. And that power by its very essence must manifest itself. And now, Jesus is showing how perfect His love is.

Now, how do you and I show Him and our neighbor how perfect our love is? Well, we're going to see what Jesus did. It says, "They were at supper, and the devil had already put it into the mind of Judas to betray Him" (John 13:2).

Now, Judas had free will. He could have said, "No." He could have, as an avaricious, greedy man, resisted that temptation. And even after he fell, he could have said he was sorry and repented and given God the glory of forgiving him. But he didn't. So now, Jesus knew that the Father had put everything into His hands, that He was soon to return to the Father. Now, we're talking about something that's very important here. Jesus knew everything that was going to happen to Him, which meant He made a decision to go through it.

You and I don't know tomorrow, and that's a good thing, because I'm not too sure you and I would choose to accept tomorrow, for the love of God. We would not choose to accept the disappointments of tomorrow or the heartaches of tomorrow or the pain of tomorrow. We don't know tomorrow, and that's a blessing. We don't know the hour of our death, and that's a blessing.

So, what St. John is saying here is that the love of Jesus for us was perfect. And it was perfect because

He knew the whole thing. He knew every pain He would endure. He knew every heartache, every disappointment, every humiliation, and He chose to do this for you.

Can you imagine anybody loving you that much? Why is it that, as an individual, when you fail, when you sin—and some of you that are not Christian that may be reading this—why is it you get so despondent and despair over your failings, your sins? Why don't you run to Jesus? When He has showed in such a perfect manner how much He loves you, why do you stay away? Why do you keep staying away? Why do you keep putting off that repentance till tomorrow? Why do you fear His justice? Why don't you just put yourself into His infinite Mercy, because He is constantly, constantly, constantly proving to you every day, in every way, how much He loves you?

And now He's proving it again, because it says here, "He got up from table, removed his outer garment and, taking a towel, wrapped it around His waist." Just imagine Our Dear Lord doing this! "He then poured water into a basin and began to wash His disciples' feet" (verses 4–5), and in such a humble way.

Can you imagine God kneeling before a sinner? All of you that are such big sinners out there, can you imagine God doing this? These men were good men but were all sinners. Even good people are sinners. We learn here and in the Gospels how much the apostles argued with one another. And how they were indignant sometimes and all of them were indignant against James and John because they wanted to be on the right and left of Jesus. These were men who had human ambitions and human frailties and weaknesses. Yet here is the Son of God kneeling in front of His apostles.

You know, some of you parents, who sometimes make some pretty bad mistakes in your life, you give your children scandal. Have you ever thought of apologizing to your children and saying to them, "I'm sorry. I have not been the man or the woman that you deserve to have"? You kind of just gloss over your sins, your anger. Have you ever really taken a child and beat him unjustly? Have you ever looked at your child and scolded him unjustly? Is the punishment you have given your children far above whatever he has done? In other words, do you vent your own personal anger and hang-ups on your children? And when you know you do, have you ever thought of just saying, "I'm sorry"?

Now, you say, "Oh, I wouldn't do that. You see, I am the parent. They are the children. I could not possibly humiliate myself."

Well, you better listen to this and listen hard, because the Son of God has knelt down before a sinner — before many sinners. These apostles were faulty people who were in need of redemption. And He knelt down before them and washed their feet.

Now, the apostles were indignant again. They said, "Lord, are You going to wash my feet?" This is Simon Peter. Simon Peter was always getting his foot in his mouth. Simon Peter was a man who constantly spoke before he thought. And I think he got himself into an awful lot of hot water. I just have that feeling that he was a man who was always speaking and then thinking.

And so, he looks at Jesus. And he says, "Are You going to wash my feet?" Well, Jesus had already washed probably everybody else's feet. And Jesus looked at Peter and He said, "Well, at the moment you don't know what I'm doing, but you will understand." And

Jesus is very patient with the man. And Peter looks at Him, and he says, "Never! You shall never wash my feet."

There he is again, always trying to do his own thing. Jesus looked at him very seriously, and He says, "Peter, if I do not wash you, you can have nothing in common with Me."

What does that mean? You know what it means? It means that it takes just as much humility to accept an apology as it does to make one. It took just as much humility on the part of the apostles to let Jesus wash their feet—and of course, God in the Person of Jesus, Who always had infinite humility, so we cannot compare degree—but it took humility for Peter and the rest of the apostles to let the Son of God wash their feet. And it took fantastic humility for Jesus, Creator and Lord and Savior, Brother and Benefactor, God, the Word Made Flesh and dwelling among us, to kneel down and wash His apostles' feet.

Do you know what this did for you and me? It took away all our excuses. We no longer have excuses for our pride. We can no longer say, "I cannot apologize, because I'm on the top. I am the leader." You can't say that. When you are so big in your own eyes that you can never say "I'm sorry" to someone you have offended, then you are not being like Jesus.

When Jesus washed these apostles' feet, what He was saying was that they were to be humble as He was humble. Jesus never asked us to do anything that He didn't do Himself first. And that's another lesson for us, isn't it? Because He's saying to Peter, "If you don't let Me do this, if you're not going to be humble, then you have nothing in common with Me."

When you find a proud Christian, they have nothing in common with Jesus. When you find an arrogant Christian, they have nothing in common with Jesus. That name or that title does you absolutely nothing. In fact, you are a scandal to the world when you're arrogant and then call yourself a Christian.

Do you know what humility is? Humility is truth. And that's a little bit confusing to some people, because sometimes pride is truth, is it not?

For example, if I were a sculptor and I sculpted a beautiful statue of somebody, and it was beautiful, it was a perfect work of art, I could look at it and say, "It is a perfect work of art," and it would be true.

So far, humility and pride are right together, right here. They are both looking at a truth. Humility can look at the statue and say, "It is a beautiful sculpture." Pride looks at it and says, "It is a beautiful sculpture."

The differences right now at this point are that humility says, "Praise God for giving me this talent." Pride says, "This talent is mine; I did it alone." No thought of God. No thought of a Supreme Being Who gave a gift to a mere man — the gift to take a rock, a stone, a piece of wood and carve it into something that's almost alive.

So, humility sees the truth and looks to God. Pride sees truth and looks to itself. Don't let the truth trip you up, because Jesus is the Truth. And when you do something that's good, you praise God for it because God gave you that talent, every talent you possess — even the gift to see.

You say, "These are my eyes!" But they were a gift.

You know, it's so sad when you see a scientist or a man with a great intelligence being arrogant or attributing everything he does to himself. It's very sad, because he could not and has not and never could give himself intelligence. God gave it to him. To use something that is a gift and pretend it was not a gift is a lie. So, pride is a lie. And humility is a truth that rises to God in humble gratitude.

Now, this is the reason why Jesus said to Peter, "Well, if you're not going to be humble, you have no part of Me." In the Kingdom, there are men and women who were once robbers and thieves and murderers and prostitutes. But there is no one in the Kingdom who is not humble. The only place where there are people full of pride in the afterlife is Hell. Hell is that place where everyone refuses to admit they're wrong.

You know, it's a frightening thing. Some people find it very difficult to admit they are ever wrong. They find it almost impossible to ever say, "I made a mistake. I mean, I really goofed. I just messed up this whole thing!" and begin again. They talk themselves out of it, or they'll look you straight in the eye and say, "I didn't do that" or just gloss over it as if it never happened.

You see, that's a great act of pride. And Hell is full of people who refuse to admit. You know what they are? They're people who are always right. That's why they cannot admit the truth. Humility is a person who's willing to admit he made a mistake. That's why

I find sometime in great, great sinners a kind of humility that some good people don't have. And I find this very hard to understand.

I sometimes wonder about the degradation of a wino in the gutter, and when you go up to him and reach out your hand, there's a kind of humility about him. Oh, it's not the right kind, but the kind of humility he has is that he knows where he's at. Down! He admits it. Sometimes, hopefully, he wants to be helped, and that's the glory of humility. The glory of humility is that beautiful childlikeness that permits us not only to know we need help but to accept that help. This is why some people cannot receive a favor. Now, they can give you something or they can do something for you, and they're very good at that. But when you try to do something for them, they feel uneasy. That's pride. Because it is a gift to give, and it is a gift to receive.

And when Our Dear Lord was being very emphatic here to Peter, He knew that Peter was going to need a lot of humility. Peter was going to take these apostles and lead them to the Kingdom. He was going to be the first one after Pentecost to go out in all boldness and look out into that crowd and say, "Men of Judea, listen to what I have to say!"

This is a man who was so afraid, he denied his Lord. Jesus knew that to have the kind of success Peter was going to have to raise the dead, to heal, to perform miracles, Peter was going to be deeply rooted in humility. He was going to have to know. And you find Peter with a great deal of humility later on.

When he cured the man at the Beautiful Gate, he said, "Why do you come to me?" He said, "Jesus healed you. The Name of Jesus healed you." So, he gave glory to God. He said, "Silver and gold I have none, but what I have, I give thee."

So, he knew he had a power. He knew God had given him a gift. When they flocked to him, he said, "Why do you come to me as if something I did helped you? It was the Name of Jesus that helped you." See the humility? Peter knew he had a gift. He knew he had a power. But he also knew where that power came from, and the acknowledgment of that power was humility.

You and I, in this life, in this particular world that you and I are living in, in this age, in this time — we must be humble. We must look at our neighbor—no matter how degrading his life is, no matter how great a sinner he is, no matter how deprived or depraved—and we must realize: "There goes me but for the grace of God." And so, we cannot judge or condemn. A humble man never judges or condemns because he knows that if he were put in similar situations, he may also fall. So, he can look. He can help. He can reach out his hand and never be condescending, always be empathetic, because he feels when his neighbors need. He knows that only God's grace keeps him from doing things much worse than he sees his neighbor doing.

And so, we see Peter here again. Peter is beginning to get the gist of it. He's beginning to understand a little bit what Jesus is trying to tell him. And now he wants to go all out.

And Peter says, "Then, Lord, not only my feet, but my hands and my head as well!" (verse 9). I mean, if it needs humility to be close to Jesus, then Peter wants the whole person to be humbled. If Jesus wants to wash his head, his hands, his feet—praise God! He was going to look at Jesus in the way that Jesus wanted him to look at Him. He wanted to be everything Jesus wanted him to be.

And Jesus says, "No one who has taken a bath needs washing, such a person is clean all over. You too are clean, though not all of you are" (verses 10–11).

You know, that's one of the saddest statements in Scripture. "You too are clean, though not all of you are." Because He knew who was going to betray Him. He knew, and He tried very hard to take Judas, to love him, to protect him, to warn him, over and over. And you see throughout the Gospels little warnings that Jesus was giving him, through His counsels to the crowd. But the man would not listen.

And He said to the apostles, "Do you understand what I have done to you? You call me Master and Lord, and rightly; so I am" (verse 13). He acknowledged His Sonship. "If I, then, the Lord and Master, have washed your feet, you must wash each other's feet" (verse 14).

Well, we don't always have that opportunity, but we can, every day, wash the feet of our neighbor by looking at him with a humble eye, never looking down on him, never looking at him with a haughty eye, never saying to him, "I would never do that," never condemning them, never looking at him with an eye of avarice, greed, envy, jealousy. Humility is that beautiful virtue that makes us so much like God, because it makes us free. It gives without counting the cost.

Humility enables us to love our neighbor, even if that neighbor doesn't love us in return. Humility enables us to see God in the least. Humility enables us to do a good deed to the least of all men and know and realize that I am doing it to Jesus—that whatever I do to my neighbor, I do to Him.

Humility is truth. It is to acknowledge your talents, to acknowledge your virtues; it is to acknowledge that God made you good, and you give all the credit to God. Humility is to use your talents for the good of the Kingdom, for the good of the people of God. To use your talents in such a way that you give of yourself totally because you want to help your neighbor, you want to be an image of God to your neighbor, you want to radiate Jesus to your neighbor. This is humility.

It's not making yourself a rug or a doormat for everyone to walk on. Humility is strong. It's a strong virtue because it is built on truth. And the truth makes you free. It is only the proud man who is enslaved.

Enslaved by his own thoughts, enslaved by himself, he is in a constant prison. He is more in a prison than any prisoner in a jail. But he is confined within the confines of his own soul.

But the humble man is totally and absolutely free. He sees his faults, and he never despairs. When he falls, he repents immediately. He's not surprised at his faults. He's only surprised he doesn't fall lower and more often. He gives credit to God for every good thing that happens to him. He sees God in the present moment. He sees God in the little joys and the big joys of his life. He sees God in pain and disappointment. And he sees God in everything. Because he sees God in everything, he's able to handle reality — the reality of life, the reality of living, the reality of pain and suffering and joy, the reality of agonies and ecstasies. He is a realist. The humble man is a realist because he is built on the rock of God.

Be humble and be truthful because God loves you.

Chapter 5

We're going to look at St. John's Gospel. If you have the Gospel with you, look at chapter 6. It's called "the Miracle of the Loaves." It's a very, very important lesson for you and me in this beautiful incident in the Lord's life.

It says, "After this" — after they had passed over the Sea of Galilee — "a large crowd followed him, impressed by the signs He gave by curing the sick," and raising the dead and delivering those from demons — they had many, many signs. "Looking up Jesus saw the crowds approaching and said to Philip, 'Where can we buy some bread for these people to eat?' He said this only to put Philip to the test" (John 6:1–6).

Now, this is an important sentence in Scripture. You know, we don't often think of Jesus doing something to test us. It says here deliberately, "He said this only to put Philip to the test." Jesus wants to know how much faith we really have in Him, how much confidence we have in His power. And poor Philip, he said, "Well, two hundred denarii will just buy enough bread to give each one a small piece," just a little bit.

Very practical. Philip was looking at the situation at hand, being very practical. And he said, "Well, two hundred denarii isn't much. A little bit for everybody."

Jesus knew what He was going to do, and He wondered what Philip would have done. Wouldn't it have been wonderful if Philip had said, "Lord, I just don't know. But You do. And You can do something about it." Wouldn't that have thrilled Jesus' heart?

Wouldn't it be a thrill if you had said that today when the Lord said, "Well, what are you going to do about the situation?" If you were just to look at Him and say, "Lord, I don't know, but You do. And I'll do whatever You tell me."

But Philip didn't. He just got very practical. And he said, "There is a small boy here with five barley loaves and two fish." Here's a little kid that brought a lunch, who's smarter than anybody. All these adults came just to hear and to sit there and enjoy Jesus, and this little kid—I bet he went and got some fishes and two loaves of bread, and he said, "Boy, I'm going to eat!" He really had brains. He said, "I'm going to eat!" He took these loaves and fishes with him.

"Jesus said to them, 'Make the people sit down'" (verse 10).

Now, St. John tells us there was plenty of grass, and St. Mark says there was tall grass there. It says there were five thousand men. Now, we're not counting women and children. So there may have been anywhere from ten thousand to fifteen thousand people in this tall grass, sitting in groups of fifty. You could easily count it.

"Then Jesus took the loaves, gave thanks, and distributed them to those who were sitting there" (verse 11). You know, that's very important. These people had gotten to the point where, had they left Jesus, they would have fainted on their way. They had been with Him a long, long time. They were sitting ready. They didn't know what was going to happen, but they trusted Him, and they knew that something would happen.

In His Sandals

You and I, when we come into situations in our life when we just don't know what to do — in fact, when there's just nothing to do! — instead of getting frustrated and angry with God and angry with our neighbor and angry with ourselves, why don't we just sit ready? Sit ready and say to God, "I knew You would do something. I know You will do something." And many times in our life, we reach those situations where we can't do anything. We just have to sit ready.

Now, He did the same with the fish, and He started to give these out, the fish and the bread. "When they had eaten enough, He said to His disciples" — and this is important, and I want you to listen to this sentence — "'Pick up the pieces left over, so that nothing is wasted'" (verse 12).

Pick up the scraps. That's what He was saying. "Go into that tall grass and pick up all those scraps." Now, you and I would have been practical like Philip. And we would have left those scraps and said, "Well, they'll make good fertilizer." We would have brushed ourselves off. We would have been litterbugs. Just leave it there. Dump it.

And Jesus said, "Go and pick up the scraps."

"So they picked them up, and filled twelve hampers with scraps left over" (verse 13).

Twelve large baskets with scraps left over. Now, these were pieces of bread and fish that people had left over after Jesus had given them this bread and fish. Some were small pieces, some had been chewed at; some were large pieces; some were on the ground in the grass; some of the people had it in their hands.

And Jesus said, "Pick it all up. Pick it up off the ground." You and I would have all kinds of sanitary reasons why we should leave it there. We would have never thought of picking up those scraps. But you see, have you ever wondered what happened to those scraps after Jesus took them and filled those twelve baskets? I bet those apostles ate those scraps for months! Did you ever, ever think about Thanksgiving dinner? I look forward to Thanksgiving dinner, except that sometimes I'm still eating it at Christmas.

One time, one January, I saw something on the table that looked quite familiar. And I said to the sisters, "What is this?" And they said, "Turkey." And I said, "Turkey! Where'd we get it?" They said, "Well, we had it left over from Thanksgiving." And I said,

"O Lord, that Thanksgiving turkey just never disappears. It gets bigger and bigger and bigger and bigger."

I think that's what happened to these twelve hampers. I bet those apostles ate fish and bread and fish and bread until it came out of their ears! But it nourished them. There was enough nourishment in those scraps to feed those apostles for days.

Do you understand the lesson? Are you kind of getting the message? If Jesus was so concerned with these scraps—and they were nothing but fish and bread—do you think the scraps in your life He's going to let go? All those things you wish you had never done, all the things you did, all the mistakes you made—do you think He's going to let any of these things go without using them for your good somehow, some way, all those scraps in your life, the things you wished had never happened? And doesn't St. Paul assure us that, for those who love God, God brings good out of everything that happens to them (Romans 8:28)?

Now, those scraps that the people and the apostles would surely like to have left there and just taken off, those scraps that they considered of no good or no use—they wanted to turn their backs on them and forget them, buried in that tall grass and never seen again. Most of you take the scraps in your life, and you permit them to just pour upon your poor soul guilt or resentment or regrets, and you live in that guilt. And Jesus is saying, "Put those scraps in a hamper, and I will make them nourish you. Your very sins will be used to keep you humble and dependent."

You know from your past what you're capable of. Let that make you depend upon Him, not discourage you. You understand from your past what you're capable of, but Jesus wants to take that and turn it around, to take that scrap you want to forget and bury. He wants to raise it up. He wants to use it to give you those gifts and those qualities and those virtues that are most like Himself.

You know, we really can't be humble unless we understand our weaknesses and how much we depend upon God for every single thing. We depend upon God to wake in the morning and to sleep at night, to eat and to sleep and to see and to feel and to hear and to touch. We need God every moment of our life, and sometimes when we forget Him, we suddenly lose these things, even for a moment, even for a day, a month, or a year.

In His Sandals

One time, I went deaf for a few days. It frightened me. Never did I realize the gift of hearing until suddenly I could no longer hear. I don't think I ever thanked God before that time for the gift of hearing. And I had wished that I had thanked Him for that gift more often. There are things in our life that we regret — your life, my life — decisions we make that are seemingly wrong decisions. But God uses those beautiful things, and I call them beautiful because after He gets through with them, they are able to nourish our souls. They teach us self-knowledge.

If I had never been impatient my whole life, I would never know what impatience was. But I have suffered from impatience and anger. And I know what it means to have to control yourself. I know! And I wish I had never felt angry or distressed. But I have. But I also know now that Jesus is going to take all those scraps in my life, and all the scraps in your life, and He will make something out of them that is so nourishing for our soul and so beautiful because of the presence of God.

And that's what was the point here. They only had two hundred denarii to feed the people. They

You know, youth look at the older people in such distress—the older people trying to be young. You know, when I see somebody eighty years old in the mall with shorts on, I think that's terrible! If they could look at themselves in a mirror to see how they look, trying to be young!

Why can't we be honest? And be what we are—old! We're getting there. But that should give us a joy. You see, the youth today are not able to look at the elderly or the senior citizens and say, "Hey! It gets better as you get older!" Or "Hey! I have something to look forward to!" They look at most old people today who are sad-sacked, disgruntled, unhappy, sour, fighting to remain in this life, acting as if there is no eternity, bitter over their age, their children, their positions, the fact that they can't do the things they used to do.

You know, the youth of today look at that, and they don't look forward to tomorrow. They don't look forward to age. You know there are a tremendous amount of suicides among our youth? It's frightening! I think all of you that are senior citizens have a beautiful mission from God, and that mission from God is to radiate the joy of the coming of the Kingdom. You're getting close to it. And if you don't look forward to it, what is a sixteen-year-old kid going to look forward to? You have to realize that if you are a senior citizen, you have an obligation to help the world, and you *can* help the world. Whether you live in a convalescent home or you live with your children or you live by yourself, you can be such a beautiful example.

If there's one thing the world needs, it's hope in the future. You see, you're an image of the future. I hope I live till I'm one hundred. I don't know how many other people wish I lived to be one hundred, but I do. Because I realize that every moment I have in time, I can love God more, I can love my neighbor more. You see, it's not a matter of whether you're sick or not sick or whether you can do something or you're famous or unheralded by the world or unknown by the world. That doesn't matter. Those are frills. The thing that matters is my capacity to know God and love God.

Let me explain it to you. For example, if you had to walk half a mile of very thin chiffon veils, and every time you love God, every time you love your neighbor, every time you do something good, every time you do anything that increases that divine nature in your soul—that grace, that divine Spirit in your soul—it's like taking away one of those chiffon veils.

Now, if you died between here and the end of the half mile, you'd see that much more of God, wouldn't you? Now, maybe with all the veils you could see God? But the more you take away a veil, the more of God you see. You'd see His beauty. You'd see His power. You'd see His mind. It's one joy after another! This is forever. It means your capacity for love is greater.

Old age is a blessing, but today we look upon it as a curse. And now they talk about doing away with old people. How hardened we have become! How terribly un-Christian! We're not like God, because we're saying it's survival of the fittest. We've taken away the beauty of old age. We look upon those in old age as if they had no wisdom, as if everyone that was old was almost senile.

Let me tell you about the senile. Don't write them off. Because if they are in a state of grace, they hold God up in the world as if they were a temple. It's your soul and my soul that are temples of the Lord. And that temple gets more and more beautiful. Don't look at the wrinkles on your face and the gray hair and your faltering steps. You look at that soul.

You know, that's what's hard, isn't it? Do you know why it's hard to be old or to admit it? It's because your soul is young. Your body is old, and your body cannot keep up with your soul. So, you feel young, but you look in the mirror, and you don't have the strength you used to have. Your body is old! It's going down, but inside is sure young because your soul is immortal. We'll never die. That's why death is so hard for us to understand. We all have an inner realization that we shall never die. That's why Jesus and the Kingdom and gentleness and principles are so important, because your whole eternity depends upon this short life.

And as we said before, know it or not, or like it or not, you shall live forever. You shall never die. Your soul will live forever. It is immortal. We have been in the mind of God before time began, and you shall live forever. It behooves you and me to keep this in mind.

You know, we should act toward the old with awe. I know they get crotchety once in a while, but you can't judge an orange by the peel. Isn't that funny? We go to a store, and we buy all the fruit by the outside peel. We look at a pear, and if it looks beautiful, we buy it. We look at an orange, and if it's real orange and big, we buy it. So, we judge and we buy entirely by appearances. And when we get home, we take off the appearance and throw it away. So, what we bought the thing for we throw away and keep the inside.

But that's what you have to do with age, with your life. So, don't bother about the appearance — sagging eyelids and jowls and wrinkles and gray hair or no hair. These things are incidents. One day that body, be it ever so decrepit, will rise. God will say, "Come forth!" and your soul will be reunited to your body, and we'll rise and be glorified, just like the Lord Jesus' Body is glorified. This is very important for you understand. So, you keep your dignity as a senior citizen, and you keep up your hope. The world needs you!

What I'm trying to bring out is that those of you who are up in your years — sixty, seventy, eighty, nineties, God has kept the best wine for you till now. Old age is that best wine, as far as your individual soul is concerned, because you have a mission in the world. Your mission is to prove to the youth of today and the middle-aged that there is a Kingdom. You look forward to going. You look forward to that Kingdom. And that this life, be it ever so burdensome to you and difficult and lonely and painful, is a joy because you're doing God's will and that you have the presence of God in your soul. That the water He gave you when He created you has been turned into the wine of His grace. And that grace has grown and grown greater and greater as you got older. That the wisdom that you've had and amassed over the years, you are willing to share with the youth.

And those of you who are younger, you look upon the old with awe and with respect, because their capacity for God has grown and is very great. Their union with God may be very, very great. And believe me, my friends, God listens to their prayers because they are full of God. And you and I must begin again to have that beautiful respect for those who are elderly. Don't look at their grouchiness and their complaining and their little organ recitals about all their sicknesses. You listen to those. They give you the opportunity to listen and to be like Jesus. They make you understand that one day you, too, will be old. And you look upon that age with great gratitude, because age is a gift from

God. It means that the longer you live, the greater a vision you will have of God, the greater capacity for glory and love.

Now, you can also lose that by being bitter, disgruntled, hateful, complaining. God has really kept the best wine until now. Your old age is that best wine. God is giving you and me the best wine in the New Testament. He has given us His Son, Who bled for us; He died for us and rose for us. There is no wine like His Precious Blood. And His Precious Blood gives you and me life everlasting. And His Precious Blood redeemed us. And we can call upon that Precious Blood whenever we are in need, to defend us from the enemy, the world, and the flesh, because in that Precious Blood, that new wine, is glory and salvation.

So, you look upon the aged with respect. Ask Jesus to give you the new wine of His grace. If you are a sinner, repent. Just as that sinner condition makes your human nature back into water, repentance and His mercy will change your sinner condition into wine just as quickly as He did this water at the Marriage of Cana.

In His Sandals

So, you look at this little story. It's not just a story. It was an incident in the Lord's life—this great woman who inaugurated it and Jesus, Who gave us the wine of grace in this New Testament. God bless you and love you.

Mother M. Angelica
(1923–2016)

Mother Mary Angelica of the Annunciation was born Rita Antoinette Rizzo on April 20, 1923, in Canton, Ohio. After a difficult childhood, a healing of her recurring stomach ailment led the young Rita on a process of discernment that ended in the Poor Clares of Perpetual Adoration in Cleveland.

Thirteen years later, in 1956, Sister Angelica promised the Lord as she awaited spinal surgery that, if He would permit her to walk again, she would build Him a monastery in the South. In Irondale, Alabama, Mother Angelica's vision took form. Her distinctive approach to teaching the Faith led to parish talks, then pamphlets and books, then radio and television opportunities.

In His Sandals

By 1980 the Sisters had converted a garage at the monastery into a rudimentary television studio. EWTN was born. Mother Angelica has been a constant presence on television in the United States and around the world for more than forty years. Innumerable conversions to the Catholic Faith have been attributed to her unique gift for presenting the gospel: joyful but resolute, calming but bracing.

Mother Angelica spent the last years of her life cloistered in the second monastery she founded: Our Lady of the Angels in Hanceville, Alabama, where she and her Nuns dedicated themselves to prayer and adoration of Our Lord in the Most Blessed Sacrament.